PAST IN PICTURES

A photographic view of
Holidays

WAYLAND

First published in 2013 by Wayland
Copyright © Wayland 2013

Wayland
338 Euston Road
London NW1 3BH

Wayland Australia
Level 17/207 Kent Street
Sydney, NSW 2000

Editor: Joyce Bentley
Concept Design: Lisa Peacock
Designer: Elaine Wilkinson
Researchers: Laura Simpson and Hester Vaizey at
The National Archives

Picture acknowledgements:
Material reproduced by courtesy of The National
Archives, London, England. www.nationalarchives.
gov.uk. Catalogue references and picture
acknowledgements Main cover: INF2-43 (1186)
'Holidays at Home' Guildford swimming pool 1943
(tl); INF2-43 (1200) 'Holidays at Home' for War
Workers Peter Pan statue, Kensington Gardens 1943
(tr); COPY1-443(ii) (574) Ladies paddling 1899 (bl);
RAIL399-53 Cromer1939 (br); Back cover: COPY1-
209 f264 Great Northern Railway, Christmas and
New Year holiday excursions, 1903 (l); RAIL399-
53 Lowestoft 1939 (r); title page: Mary Evans
Picture Library/Francis Frith; p2: Getty Images/
John Drysdale; p3: RAIL399-53 Lowestoft 1939; p4:
COPY1-26 (368) The Child's Holiday ABC, 1874;
p5: Getty Images; p6: COPY1-439 (61) Children in
the grounds of Hornchurch Holiday Home 1899;
p7: COPY1-443(ii) (574) Ladies paddling 1899;
p8: Illustrated London News Ltd/Mary Evans; p9:
COPY1-209 f264 Great Northern Railway, Christmas
and New Year holiday excursions, 1903; p10: COPY1-
465 Mary Wheatland, the Bognor bathing woman,
1903 Photographer William Marsh; p11: Mary Evans
Picture Library/Francis Frith; p12: COPY1-234 (257)
GWR Holiday Haunts 1905; p13: Vintage Images/
Alamy; p14: EXT1-315 Pt10 (2) No Holidays; p15:
Mary Evans Picture Library; p16: RAIL253-76
Holiday crowds at Paddington 1929; p17: Popperfoto/
Getty Images; p18: RAIL399-53 Cromer1939; p19:
RAIL399-53 Lowestoft 1939; p20: RAIL399-53
Butlins Holiday Camp Skegness 1939; p21: NSC5-75
Spend your hoilday at home and Save your holiday
money 1942; p22: INF2-43 (1186) 'Holidays at Home'
Guildford swimming pool 1943; p23: INF2-43 (1198)
'Holidays at Home' for War Workers Hyde Park Lido
1943; p24: INF2-43 (1200) 'Holidays at Home' for
War Workers Peter Pan statue, Kensington Gardens
1943; p25: INF2-108 (13) Holiday resorts recruitment
advertisement 1946; p26: INF13-233 (11) Staggered
Holidays help everybody 1950s; p27: CMary Evans
Picture Library; p28: Getty Images/John Drysdale;
p29: Bettmann/CORBIS

A cataloguing record for this title is available at the
British Library.

Dewey number: 306.4'8125-dc23

ISBN: 978 0 7502 7969 7

Printed in China

Wayland is a division of Hachette Children's Books,
an Hachette UK company
www.hachette.co.uk

1st section

Contents

Introduction

In this book we look at photographs and other kinds of images of holidays, from Victorian times up until the 1960s. We examine these images for clues about the past and see what we can learn from them about the way people used to live. On pages 30-31, you can find some questions and points to explore, to encourage further discussion of the pictures.

1874

← Children go on holiday in horse-drawn carriages.

← Grand tours of Europe became fashionable for wealthy people during the 16th century, but it was not until Victorian times that ordinary people began 'going on holiday'. One of the most popular destinations was the seaside. In this image, children are going on holiday in large carriages called charabancs (pronounced shar-a-bangs).

1890

↓ Tourists queue up to visit the Tower of London

↑ From the late 19th century, there was a growth in 'heritage tourism': people travelling to visit sites of historical interest. Historical cities such as London, Bath, Oxford, Edinburgh and York attracted many visitors, both from Britain and from abroad.

⬇ **These children are staying at a holiday home.**

↑ Some wealthy Victorians were inspired by a desire to improve the lives of the poor. This house in Staffordshire was built in the 1890s by the Duke of Sutherland so that poor children in the local area could have a place to go on holiday. It provided accomodation for fifteen children.

↓ These women are paddling in the sea.

↑ In the Victorian era, it was not considered respectable for men or women to wear revealing swimming costumes, so many opted to paddle in their ordinary clothes. Beach resorts often had bathing machines – wooden carts pulled into the sea by horses – so bathers could get into the water without exposing themselves.

← This is an advert for low-price bank holiday railway trips.

← Bank holidays are public holidays when banks are closed and most people are allowed the day off work. They were first introduced in Britain in 1871. The politician who created them was called Sir John Lubbock. People were so grateful that for a while they called them St Lubbock's Days. Bank holiday weekends have traditionally been a time when people go away for short holidays.

→ Adverts encouraged people to take railway trips during their holidays.

→ The railways changed the lives of millions of people, making it possible to travel cheaply and quickly over long distances. People made long excursions and also took day trips, for example to sporting events. Railway tourism first took off in 1850, when Britain had 11,000 km of rail track. By 1900, this had increased to 35,000 km of track.

9

→ Mary Wheatland was a famous lady from Bognor Regis, who taught children to swim.

→ Mary Wheatland (1835–1924) rented out bathing machines on the seafront at Bognor Regis. An expert swimmer, she received medals for the many lives she saved. Crowds would gather to watch her swim in her serge suit. They would applaud as she stood upside down so only her boots protruded from the sea.

1904

↓ **Children enjoy donkey rides on the beach at Weymouth.**

↑ Donkey rides have been a tradition at seaside resorts since the late 19th century. They take place on sandy beaches during the summer season. Usually, children ride the donkeys in groups at walking pace. The donkeys often have their names printed on their harnesses.

← This railway advert suggests lots of places for holidaymakers to stay.

← By the early 1900s, there was a large and growing tourist industry in Britain. As well as seaside resorts, other places were offering themselves as holiday destinations, including country houses and farms. Health resorts, such as the spa towns of Bath and Harrogate, had been popular with wealthy tourists since the 18th century.

← An elderly couple with their daughter on board an ocean liner.

← The first ships to offer a regular passenger service with an emphasis on comfort were a fleet of sailing ships owned by the Black Ball Line, which began operating in 1818. In 1891, the *Augusta Victoria* offered passengers the first 'cruise', with fine dining, well-appointed staterooms and stop-offs at interesting places. Ships were no longer just a form of transport, but a holiday destination in themselves.

← During World War I factory workers were discouraged from taking holidays.

← Munitions are bombs, weapons and ammunition. The government was desperate to maintain the supply of munitions to the soldiers on the front line, so it urged munitions workers to keep working throughout the year. The workers were encouraged to see it as their patriotic duty not to take a holiday.

1920s

A group of people set off on holiday in two charabancs.

On page 4, we saw some horse-drawn charabancs. By the early 20th century, these vehicles had become motorised. They were usually open-topped, but had a canvas folding hood in case of rain. Charabancs reached the peak of their popularity during the 1920s, after which they were replaced by buses and coaches.

↓ Holiday-goers crowd the platform at Paddington Station in London.

↑ Paddington Station has been the London terminus for journeys to and from the west of England since it was founded in 1838. The present station, with its arched roofs of wrought iron and glass, was built by the great engineer Isambard Kingdom Brunel in 1854. Holiday destinations served by Paddington include Bath Spa, Bristol, Cardiff, Exeter, Gloucester, Hereford and Oxford.

1938

↓ Children in the Cotswolds celebrate May Day by dancing around a maypole.

↑ May Day is a traditional spring holiday in Britain. Celebrations include Morris dancing, crowning a May Queen and maypole dancing. There are different kinds of maypole dance. Sometimes people perform circle dances around a decorated maypole. In another version, each dancer holds a coloured ribbon attached to the pole, which they wind around it, and then unwind, as they dance.

← These children are having fun on the beach.

← This photograph was taken on the beach at Cromer, in Norfolk, which has been a seaside resort since the early 19th century. A pier was opened there in 1901, with a pavilion added in 1905 that hosted concerts and shows. The Pavilion Theatre has been one of the major attractions at Cromer ever since.

1939

⬇ People are sitting on deckchairs on the beach.

↑ Lowestoft, in Suffolk, has wide, sandy beaches and two piers. It has been a popular destination for holidaymakers since the railway arrived there in the mid-19th century. Deckchairs were originally developed in the 1860s for use on ships. The hiring out of deckchairs in seaside resorts became customary in the early 20th century.

1939

↓ Holiday camps became popular in the 1930s.

↑ Billy Butlin opened his first holiday camp in Skegness in 1936. Holiday camps were quite a new idea then: they provided customers with chalet-style accomodation, meals and entertainment all on one site. They were tremendously popular and by 1939 there were around 200 holiday camps in Britain.

→ During World War II, people were urged not to go on holiday.

→ War changed the way people spent their holidays. Trains were needed for transporting soldiers and military supplies. It was also safer for people to stay at home. The government launched its 'Holidays at Home' programme, to encourage people not to travel. Not everyone was deterred, however. Resorts such as Blackpool remained very popular during the war.

SPEND YOUR HOLIDAY AT HOME and SAVE YOUR HOLIDAY MONEY ...put it into WAR SAVINGS

↓ People are having fun at an outdoor swimming pool.

↑ As part of the Holidays at Home programme, events were put on in local parks and town halls, including dances, sports tournaments, funfairs and concerts. The idea was that if people were entertained at home, they wouldn't feel the need to go away.

↑ The Serpentine Lido in Hyde Park was opened in 1930. Lidos – open-air swimming pools – were very popular during the 1930s and 40s, when 169 were built across the country. Many are still in use today.

↓ Children gather around the statue of Peter Pan in Kensington Gardens.

↑ During the war, children were kept entertained during the holidays with trips to local parks. Entertainments were offered, including puppet shows, games, sports events and swimming galas. Some employers even set up holiday camps for workers and their families.

→ This advert is calling on people to come and work in holiday resorts

→ When the war was over, people were desperate to go on holiday again. The barbed wire (put up to deter German invaders) was taken off the beaches on the south and east coasts, and it was boomtime once again for Britain's seaside resorts. This led to a huge demand for workers to staff the hotels and guesthouses.

JOBS AT HOLIDAY RESORTS

for men and women

Here's a chance for those who live in towns and cities to enjoy a change of air and scene in a well-paid full-time job this summer while waiting for permanent work in their home towns.

Cooks, Cook-generals, Waiters, Waitresses, Kitchen-Maids, House-maids, Pantry Maids and similar workers with or without experience are required in thousands for seasonal work this summer at Britain's holiday resorts. Lack of experience is not an obstacle, and there is a wide choice of jobs for men and women.

Call in at your local Employment Exchange and make enquiries. They will give you full details of these summer resort jobs.

ASK if you are eligible for FREE FARE, TRAVELLING ALLOWANCE and SETTLING-IN GRANT

Workers from certain areas who undertake to stay for the season will receive Free Fares to the job, Travelling Allowances and Settling-in Grant. For workers with dependants, Lodging allowances may also be payable. While away these workers would be considered for suitable jobs by the Employment Exchange in their home area. Details of these arrangements are given in Leaflet M 334 obtainable from the local Employment Exchange.

ISSUED BY **THE MINISTRY OF LABOUR AND NATIONAL SERVICE**

← A poster telling people to avoid taking their holidays at busy times.

← Because so many people went on holiday during the peak season of July and August, the country's industrial production fell dramatically during those months. So a campaign was launched to encourage people to take their summer holidays at other times of the year.

1950s

↓ Campers set up their tents in an orchard.

↑ Camping holidays began in the late 19th century. The first campsite opened in 1894 on the Isle of Man, and the first campers' handbook was published in 1908. However, it wasn't until the 1950s and 1960s that camping really took off. As camping equipment improved, people came to see it as a cheap and fun way to spend a holiday.

1962

↓ A group of beginners receive a skiing lesson at a resort on Cairngorm, Scotland.

↑ Skiing package holidays began in 1903, when skier and writer Sir Arnold Lunn began offering ski trips, including travel and accommodation, to the Swiss Alps. Chair lifts arrived in the 1930s, and by the 1960s, ski resorts had become popular holiday destinations. The ski resort on Cairngorm was established in 1960. By the 1980s, it was attracting thousands of visitors each year.

⬇ **An air stewardess offers refreshments to passengers on board an aeroplane.**

↑ During the mid-20th century, holidays changed dramatically with the arrival of cheap air flights. The first package holidays – combining flight, transfers and hotel accommodation – began in 1950. By the 1960s, millions of people were holidaying abroad each year. As a result, British seaside resorts suffered a major decline.

Questions to Ask and Points to Explore

Picture on page 4

Questions to ask

1. Imagine leaving your home for the first time to go on a seaside holiday in a horse-drawn charabanc. Describe your excitement and any anxieties you might feel.

2. How do you think this compares to a modern-day journey to the seaside? List the advantages and disadvantages of travelling this way.

Points to explore

Design: artwork, typography
Content: horses, vehicles, people, clothing, countryside, buildings

Picture on page 5

Questions to ask

1. The Tower of London was once used as a prison. Can you name any of its famous prisoners?

2. Do you know the name for the devices at the top of the towers and what their function is?

Points to explore

Background: architectural style of building: battlements; flag; windows, towers, domes
People: number; clothing

Picture on page 6

Questions to ask

1. Why do you think the children have been given the same clothing to wear?

2. Does this clothing look comfortable and practical?

3. How do you think they will they feel leaving this house and going back to their normal lives?

Points to explore

Background: house, grounds
People: age, gender, clothing

Picture on page 7

Questions to ask

1. In Victorian times, popular entertainments at seaside resorts included watching Punch and Judy puppet shows, eating ice cream, riding on donkeys, building sandcastles with a bucket and spade, eating fish and chips, and watching singers, dancers or comedians at a music hall. How is this different from today's seaside experience?

Points to explore

Background: beach, crowds, changing huts, buildings
People: gender, age, clothing, hats

Picture on page 8

Questions to ask

1. Why was the introduction of bank holidays good news for the railway companies?

2. On what day of the week do bank holidays usually fall?

3. Can you work out the date of the bank holiday referred to in this poster?

Points to explore

Design: typography; layout; effectiveness
Content: name of advertiser; destinations

Picture on page 9

Questions to ask

1. This advert has been produced by the Great Northern Railway, a company that no longer exists. Find out a little about the history of this company. When did it operate and what cities did its trains travel to?

Points to explore

Design: artwork, typography, purpose, effectiveness
Content: text; people: age, gender, clothing

Picture on page 10

Questions to ask

1. In about 1923, the bathing machines at Bognor were replaced by beach huts, placed at the back of the beach. Eventually, these also disappeared. Why do you think these changes occurred?

2. Mary Wheatland saved over thirty lives during her long career. What sort of people perform this job now?

Points to explore

Person: clothing; hat, medals

Picture on page 11

Questions to ask

1. How does the children's clothing differ from those of modern beachgoers? Do they look comfortable?

2. Why do you think donkey rides have declined in popularity?

Points to explore

Background: architecture, donkeys, beach
People: gender; clothing; headgear

Picture on page 12

Questions to ask

1. What do you think a 'health resort' is? How does it differ from a 'pleasure resort'? What sort of people might go there?

2. What is a boarding house and why would people stay in one?

Points to explore

Design: typography, intention of advert, effectiveness

Picture on page 13

Questions to ask

1. In 1910, ocean liners did not offer as many facilities as today, but people enjoyed sitting on deck and taking the sea air. Does this couple look happy to be there? Do you think it might be a little cold?

Points to explore

Background: deck, windows, shutters, chairs, blankets, magazine
People: ages, clothing, hats, headscarf

Picture on page 14

Questions to ask

1. Do you think this poster would have encouraged munitions workers not to take holidays? If so, why do you think it is effective?

2. Fritz was a name given to German troops by the British during World Wars I and II. The Germans had a name for the British troops. Do you know what it was? See if you can find out.

Points to explore

Design: artwork, typography, intention, effectiveness
Content: depiction of German soldiers; uniforms, sword

Picture on page 15

Questions to ask

1. Charabancs were often made so that the passenger part could be separated from the driver's section. The passenger part would be taken off during the winter. Why do you think that was?

2. The rear seats of these charabancs have been raised, so the passengers at the back are higher up. Why do you think that is?

Points to explore

Background: charabancs: wheels, steps, windscreen, body shape
People: number; clothing; hats

Picture on page 16

Questions to ask

1. What can you say about the fashions of the late 1920s by looking at this photo?

2. Do you think this train has just arrived or is about to depart?

Points to explore

Background: station architecture; signs; clock; platform kiosk
People: clothing; ages; size of crowd

Picture on page 17

Questions to ask

1. What part of the town do you think the maypole dance is being held? Why did they choose this place?

2. The musician on the left has bells on his trousers. What are these for? What kind of music do you associate fiddlers with?

Points to explore

Background: architecture, town square, pole
People: spectators; dancers; fiddler; clothing; age; gender

Picture on page 18

Questions to ask

1. What are the little huts at the back of the beach used for?

2. How does this differ from a modern beach scene?

Points to explore

Background: boats, huts
People: swimming costumes, clothing, hairstyles

Picture on page 19

Questions to ask

1. Why do you think folding wooden chairs are called deckchairs?

2. Why has a high wall been built at the back of the beach?

3. Look at how the people are dressed. How does this compare with beachware today?

Points to explore

Background: sea wall, staircase, pier, pavilion, deckchairs, groynes
People: number, activities, clothing

Picture on page 20

Questions to ask

1. Typical 1930s holiday camp entertainments included ballroom dancing, bingo, fortune telling and a photographic studio. Compare these to activities offered by modern holiday centres.

2. Why do you think holiday camps declined in popularity from the 1970s?

Points to explore

Background: architecture; fountains; swimming pool; slogan (Our true intent is all for your delight)
People: ages; swimming costume styles

Picture on page 21

Questions to ask

1. What are the drawings in this poster trying to show? Can you identify what each activity is?

2. War savings were a means by which the government could raise money for the war effort. People would buy 'government bonds' and the government would then pay them interest. Is this poster effective? What images might a similar poster use today?

Points to explore

Design: style of artwork; typography; intention; effectiveness
Content: slogan; people: activities, clothing

Picture on page 22

Questions to ask

1. What does this photograph, taken in Guildford, Surrey, tell us about the success of the Holidays at Home initiative?

2. How would this picture differ from one taken of the same scene in the early 20th century?

Points to explore

Background: swimming pool; diving board; slide; park
People: sunbathers, swimmers; clothes; swimming costumes; hairstyles

Picture on page 23

Questions to ask

1. Try to imagine what the young man and woman might be speaking about and try to write a caption for this photograph. They might be war workers on their day off. Perhaps they're not allowed to say what they do.

Points to explore

Background: Serpentine Lido; boats; park
People: expressions, mood, genders, clothing, hairstyles

Picture on page 24

Questions to ask

1. Who is the boy at the top of this statue?

2. The boy is the hero of a number of books. The author of these books also commissioned the statue. What was the author's name?

Points to explore

Background: lake, statue, trees
People: expressions, poses, activity; gender; clothing

Picture on page 25

Questions to ask

1. What do you think of this advertisement? Do you think it will attract people? How could it be improved?

2. A cook-general was a domestic servant who did cooking and housework. Do you know what a pantry maid is?

3. Why do you think they are so keen for people to come and work at the resorts?

Points to explore

Design: typography; layout; artwork

Content: meaning of: 'Employment Exchange', 'Travelling Allowances', 'Settling-in Grant'

Picture on page 26

Questions to ask

1. Why are people being asked to take their holidays in June and September?

2. What method of persuasion is being used here?

3. Why might people with children find it hard to take holidays in June and September?

4. Why have they used images of children riding donkeys?

Points to explore

Design: artwork; typography; layout
Content: donkey; children: expressions, clothing

Picture on page 27

Questions to ask

1. What are this family busy doing?

2. Have tent designs changed much since the 1950s?

Points to explore

Background: trees, field, fence
People: age, gender, clothing

Picture on page 28

Questions to ask

1. As skiing developed as a sport, an industry grew up to supply skiers with equipment and distinctive warm and colourful clothing. How do the clothes these people are wearing compare to those worn by skiers today?

2. The instructor in this photo is from a European ski resort. Why do you think there weren't so many British instructors in 1962?

Points to explore

Background: mountains, snow, clouds
People: clothing, boots, hats, sunglasses, skis, poles

Picture on page 29

Questions to ask

1. How does this differ from aeroplanes today?

2. Does this photo look posed? What do you think its purpose was?

Points to explore

Background: aircraft interior; seats, overhead lockers, trolley, coffee dispenser; cup
People: expressions; uniform; clothing; hairstyles

Some suggested answers can be found on the Wayland website www.waylandbooks.co.uk.

Further Information

Books

At the Seaside *(What Was It Like in the Past?)* by Louise and Richard Spilsbury (Heinemann Library, 2003)
The Seaside *(Changing Times)* by Ruth Thomson (Franklin Watts, 2004)
Seaside Holidays *(The Story of)* by Anita Ganeri (Raintree, 2008)
Seaside Holidays *(Ways Into History)* by Sally Hewitt (Franklin Watts, 2012)
Vacations and Holidays *(How Things have Changed)* by Jon Richards (Chrysalis Education, 2005)
Victorian Seaside Holidays *(Life in the Past)* by Mandy Ross (Heinemann Library, 2005)

Websites

http://www.bbc.co.uk/history/british/victorians/seaside_01.shtml
http://www.butlinsredcoats.com
http://www.nationalarchives.gov.uk/imagelibrary/holidays-and-travel-showcase.htm

http://www.piers.org.uk
http://www.seasidehistory.co.uk
http://www.lidos.org.uk

Glossary

accommodation A room or rooms, or a building, in which people may live or stay.

agricultural To do with farming.

ammunition A supply of bullets or shells.

bathing machine A wheeled hut drawn to the edge of the sea, used for changing in and swimming from.

Beefeater A Yeoman Warder or Yeoman of the Guard at the Tower of London.

campaign An organised course of action to achieve a particular goal.

chalet A wooden house or cottage with overhanging eaves, typically found in the Swiss Alps.

charabanc An early form of bus, used typically for pleasure trips. From the French char-á-bancs – 'carriage with benches'.

excursion A short journey or trip, especially for leisure.

gala A social occasion featuring special events, such as a swimming competition.

government bonds Certificates issued by the government promising to repay borrowed money at a fixed rate of interest at a specified time.

groyne A low wall or sturdy timber barrier built out into the sea from a beach to prevent erosion and drifting.

guesthouse A private house offering accommodation to paying guests.

health resort A holiday destination for people that offers to restore their health and/or encourage them to develop healthy habits.

heritage tourism The organisation and operation of holidays and visits to places of historical and cultural interest.

industrial Relating to industry – that is, the processing of raw materials and the manufacture of goods in factories.

lido A public, open-air swimming pool or lake for swimming in.

motorised Equipped with a motor.

munitions Military weapons, ammunition and equipment.

package holiday A holiday organised by a travel agent, with transportation, accommodation and sometimes meals included in the price.

patriotic Having or expressing devotion to one's country.

pavilion A building or tent used for a specific purpose, in particular a summerhouse or decorative building used as a shelter in a park or garden, or one used for concerts and theatrical performances.

peak season The time of year when there is maximum activity or demand for services.

resort A popular destination for holidays or recreation.

serge A durable woollen fabric.

spa town A town containing a mineral spring considered to have health-giving properties.

terminus a railway or bus terminal.

tourism The commercial organisation and operation of holidays and visits to places of interest.

World War I A war (1914–1918) in which the Central Powers (Germany, Austria-Hungary, Turkey and Bulgaria) were defeated by an alliance of Britain, France, Russia, Italy, the USA and others.